W9-CRI-019

"After a lifetime of addiction to Italian food, I had no idea you could do so much with mayonnaise!"

—JAY LENO, HOST OF
THE TONIGHT SHOW WITH JAY LENO

"A very funny, nostalgic culinary trip through WASPland...chock full of sociological information."

—LETITIA BALDRIGE, AUTHOR OF LETITIA BALDRIGE'S
COMPLETE GUIDE TO EXECUTIVE MANNERS

"This book took me to those days of the Harvard crew team, drinking martinis and eating chipped cream beef...oh, wait a minute...that wasn't me."

—ELLEN DEGENERES, ACTRESS

This book belongs to:

*"Ask not what you can do for your country . . .
ask what's for lunch."*

THE WASP COOKBOOK

ALEXANDRA WENTWORTH

WARNER 🅦 TREASURES®
Published by Warner Books
A Time Warner Company

Copyright © 1997 by Alexandra Wentworth
All rights reserved.

Warner Treasures® name and logo are registered
trademarks of Warner Books, Inc.
1271 Avenue of the Americas, New York, NY 10020

A Time Warner Company

Printed in the United States of America
First Printing: October 1997
10 9 8 7 6 5 4 3 2 1

ISBN: 0-446-91210-7

Book design by Flag
Illustrations by John Hart

This book is dedicated to my Poppy,
Eric Wentworth (Harvard 1954).

CONTENTS

INTRODUCTION

SPRING

SUMMER

Autumn

Winter

Epilogue

NEITHER FISH NOR FOWL
An Introduction to WASP Cooking

WASP   wosp (n.) . . . 2. Often disparaging. Such an American considered to be a member of the conservative, wealthy, and privileged upper class that formerly dominated U.S. society (White Anglo-Saxon Protestant).

— *WEBSTER'S DICTIONARY*

Growing up as a WASP in America, it was surprising to me that WASP ethnic cuisine seemed so unrecognized and practically nonexistent to the rest of the country. I tried desperately, up and down the Eastern Seaboard, to find a true WASP restaurant, but all the candidates I encountered had either added too much hummus or raw fish to their menus or else these establishments were secretly run (like Sarabeth's) by non-WASPs. I then took the search to bookstores. Looking for WASP cookbooks usually resulted in the bookstore owner's laughing so uproariously I was forced to escape walking backward and at a brisk pace. I even went to public libraries—but I couldn't find a thing, not even under "Goyim Cuisine." I didn't expect the Mayflower to bring over such culinary masterpieces that would cause the Sorbonne and the Cordon Bleu to stand up and salute, but a little recognition—at least for the Triscuit—would be appreciated. Obviously, I'm not expecting any I ♥ WASPs bumper stickers any time soon. However, this is what prompted me to track down some old prep school chums (off doing graduate work at Cornell, having babies in Bedford Hills, or in prison for insider trading) to collect their family recipes and cooking secrets.

I discovered that, because most food is prepared for WASPs at the country club or by their help, most recipes were not written down in any kind of organized text. Of course, occasionally, you can find recipes on the back of a Crane's stationery envelope or a yellow index card stuffed into an old Architectural Digest magazine. But for the most part, WASP cuisine has survived almost entirely through an oral tradition handed down from mothers to daughters or from butler to butler.

And so with this book, a gathering of old WASP recipes tied together in a neat bow, I hope to unveil the mystique of the WASPs and their food tradition in hopes that it, too, can be recognized in some of the world's gastronomic texts, or at least by other ethnic groups that share this mixing bowl of American food tradition.

Alexandra Wentworth

"The chief objection to the New England Puritans, of course, is not that they burned Indians at the stake, but that they cursed the country with crude cookery and uneatable victuals."

—H. L. MENCKEN

SPRING

Barn Party

Easter Supper

Derby Day

Baby Shower Brunch

Mother's Day Lunch

Bridal Tea

The WASP Wedding

Annual Family Meeting Tea

BARN PARTY

—✦—

Nothing is more exciting after a long, cold, East Coast winter than opening up the barn at the country house at the first signs of spring. Barns have become a decorative symbol of the country life, sort of life-size folk art. They are generally a place for weekend parties or for storing the vintage Mercedes. (They don't usually house farm equipment—I giggle at the thought.) Every spring we would drive in our convertibles up to Cornwall, Connecticut, for the most lively barn party of all. There would be square dancing or fox-trotting until the adults retired, then daiquiris and a thorough blaring of the Rolling Stones until the sun came up.

SPRING CHICKEN POTPIES
SERVES 6

—✦—

I like to serve these potpies in small clay flower pots. Now sometimes, because the flower pots are so deep, the pies don't cook through. But WASPs won't care—the point is, it's cute!

4	5-ounce cans chunk white chicken
4	10-ounce cans creamy potato soup
4	large carrots, diced
24	large mushrooms, quartered
4	cups diced celery
1	cup green peas
6	10-ounce packages pie crust mix

Preheat the oven to 400° F.

Combine the chicken and potato soup in a very large mixing bowl. In a large saucepan, combine the carrots, mushrooms, and celery. Cover with water, bring to a boil, reduce heat, and simmer for 10 minutes. Add carrot mixture to chicken and soup. Add peas.

Prepare pie crusts according to package instructions. Fashion the crusts on the inside of clean 4–5-inch high flower pots. Pour in mixture to within 2 inches of the top. Cover each pot with some of the remaining pie crust and puncture top crusts with a fork. Place pots on cookie sheets and bake for 1 hour or until crusts are nicely browned.

Note: Make sure to ask your local nursery if the flower pots are ovenproof.

GARDENER'S SALAD
SERVES 8–10

Best if bought from local farmers; ask your gardener where.

2   heads Boston lettuce
1   bunch red oak leaf lettuce
1   bunch watercress
2   baskets vine-ripened cherry tomatoes
2   fresh cucumbers, thinly sliced
2   bunches baby carrots, peeled
1   15-ounce bottle Newman's Own Salad Dressing (see Note)

Wash and dry the lettuce and watercress (no one likes to crunch down on dirt, even if it does indicate fresh lettuce). Combine all salad ingredients in a large wooden bowl. Pour dressing on top and toss gingerly.

Note: Newman's Own dressing is a must in any good WASP pantry. It's delicious and is used not only for salads but also as a marinade for fish, chicken, and steak. WASPs pour it on everything, and the proceeds go to charity (good for the conscience).

PURITAN PUFF
SERVES 6–8

4	cups soft white bread crumbs
2	quarts milk, scalded
1	cup granulated sugar
6	tablespoons butter, melted
6	eggs, lightly beaten
1	teaspoon salt
2	teaspoons vanilla extract
1	cup raisins
2½	cups miniature marshmallows

Preheat the oven to 375° F. Lightly butter a 6 x 9-inch or 9-inch square baking dish.

Soak the bread crumbs in the hot milk and cool slightly. Add the sugar, butter, eggs, salt, vanilla, and raisins. Pour the mixture over the marshmallows in the baking dish. Bake for 1 hour, or until top is lightly browned.

EASTER SUPPER

—✣—

WASPs will always acknowledge the religious calendar because every holiday is, quite frankly, an excuse for a social event. And what makes Easter so celebrated is, of course, the rising up of Christ. But more importantly, it's fashion! WASPs love to dress in their Easter finery—Easter bonnets, Moms in their extra-large straw hats with fuchsia ribbons, children in baby Dior lace dresses, and Dads in yellow ties. After church, where everyone gets parched from bellowing "Onward Christian Soldiers," the egg hunt almost always concludes with the colored eggs in the Labradors' mouths. And then there's Easter supper. WASPs always have plenty of vodka tonics and martinis, as well as the blood of Christ—a fine Lafite Rothschild 1985.

SPRING ROAST HAM
SERVES 18–20

—✣—

Now if you were a good **WASP** and did your pig killing in January or February, then you would have a succulent ham by now. If not, buy a 10-pound whole ham from your local butcher.

Preheat the oven to 300° F.

Place the ham in an uncovered roasting pan and bake for 2½ hours. Remove the rind, but be careful not to remove any fat. Cut the fat surface into a diamond pattern. Place a whole clove in the center of each diamond. Spread pineapple glaze (recipe follows) on the ham and return it to the oven for another 45 minutes.

PINEAPPLE GLAZE

MAKES ENOUGH FOR 1 WHOLE HAM

1	cup packed brown sugar
3	teaspoons cornstarch
1	teaspoon dry mustard
2	cups crushed pineapple

Blend ingredients in a medium mixing bowl. Spread over baked ham.

CAULIFLOWER WITH HOLLANDAISE SAUCE
SERVES 6–8

Cauliflower has been nicknamed the **WASP** of vegetables, probably because it's colorless, tasteless, and bland. The hollandaise sauce, however, does add flavor. In fact, you can always tell the non-**WASP** guest because he's the one pouring hollandaise sauce over the whole plate.

1	head cauliflower
4	egg yolks
¼	cup heavy cream
½	teaspoon salt
¼	cup lemon juice
1	cup butter, cut into pieces

Remove the leaves from the cauliflower head and cut away any stalk. Soak for 30 minutes in cold water (head down). Boil in salted water (head up) for 20 minutes or until soft.

Prepare the sauce.
MAKES ABOUT ½ CUP

In the top of a double boiler, beat the egg yolks and cream until thick and lightly colored. Blend in salt. Place top of double boiler over hot water. Add lemon juice. Cook over low heat while beating with a whisk until sauce is the consistency of thick cream.

Remove double boiler from heat, leaving top in place. Beat in butter until thoroughly melted and blended in. Pour over cooked cauliflower.

PEAS AND ONIONS
SERVES 6–8

4   15-ounce cans French peas, drained
1   10-ounce jar pearl onions, drained
Dab of butter
Salt and pepper
1   teaspoon sherry

Combine the peas and onions in a large saucepan. Heat through and add butter and salt and pepper to taste. Add sherry and serve hot.

DERBY DAY

Derby Day is the day of the infamous Kentucky Derby horse race in Louisville, Kentucky. It is a great **WASP** tradition because it combines all of their favorite things: horses, bourbon, socializing, bourbon, competition, bourbon, and did I mention? Bourbon!

MINT JULEP
MAKES 16–20 DRINKS

20 lemons

4 cups granulated sugar

3 cups water

40 sprigs of mint

Ice cubes

8–10 cups sour mash bourbon whiskey

Squeeze the lemons, reserving the rinds. In a large heavy saucepan, dissolve 3 cups of the sugar in the water, then add the lemon rinds and cook over medium heat until the liquid becomes syrupy, approximately 15 minutes. Cool.

Place the remaining 1 cup sugar on a plate. Rub

the lemon rinds on the rims of the glasses and then invert. Dip the glasses into the sugar to create the signature sugared rims. Place a bunch of mint sprigs on the bottom of each glass and fill with ice cubes. Divide the lemon juice and syrup equally among the glasses. Add ½ cup bourbon per glass. Garnish with more mint sprigs.

BINKEY'S BOURBON NIPS
MAKES 12–16 BALLS

3	cups vanilla wafers
1¼	cups pecans
1¼	cups confectioners' sugar
¾	tablespoon cocoa powder
3	tablespoons light corn syrup
6	tablespoons light bourbon

Grind the wafers and pecans in a food processor. Blend in 1 cup of the sugar and the remaining ingredients. Roll into balls about 1 inch in diameter and then roll in remaining confectioners' sugar. Place in a container for at least 24 hours before serving.

BOURBON PIE

SERVES 8–10

9-inch unbaked pie shell

3   eggs

1   cup granulated sugar

½   teaspoon salt

⅓   cup melted butter

1   cup light corn syrup

1   cup pecan halves

3   tablespoons bourbon whiskey

Preheat the oven to 450° F.

Bake the pie crust only partially for about 7 minutes. Reduce heat to 375°.

Combine all remaining ingredients in a large bowl and beat well. Pour into pie shell and bake for 50 minutes. Serve warm or cold.

BABY SHOWER BRUNCH

—✦—

A baby shower is not only an occasion to celebrate the newest member of the family but also a time when a nervous new mother can learn from the other ladies how to get into the right play group and when to start the baby's Harvard application. Helpful tips on which Ivy League school to donate a library to can be far more helpful than fifteen silver Tiffany rattles. And it's important to start the trust fund while the baby's still prenatal. Be sure to have plenty of fresh orange juice and champagne on hand. For the older women, chilled vodka is a must—they'll mix it with anything or pretend it's just ice water.

GINGER ALE FRUIT SALAD
SERVES 15–20 (WOMEN)

—✦—

6	tablespoons unflavored gelatin	3 ·	cups white and purple grapes
1	cup cold water	3	cups cut bananas
1½	cups boiling water	3	cups chopped apples
¾	cup lemon juice	6	cups sectioned oranges
6	tablespoons sugar		
3	cups ginger ale		

Soak the gelatin in cold water for 5 minutes, then dissolve in boiling water. Add the lemon juice, sugar, and ginger ale. Chill briefly.

When ginger ale mixture begins to thicken, fold in fruit, turn into molds, and chill. Serve on tea plates with sliced oranges.

PINK AND BLUE PIE
SERVES 8–10

4 eggs

1⅓ cups light cream

1 teaspoon salt

Pinch of pepper

¾ pound smoked bacon

9-inch unbaked pie shell

2 cups grated blue cheese or Jarlsberg cheese

Preheat the oven to 350° F.

Combine the eggs, cream, salt, and pepper in a medium bowl. Fry the bacon until crisp; let cool, then crumble. Add crumbled bacon to egg mixture.

On the bottom of the pie shell, sprinkle the grated cheese. Pour the egg mixture on top and bake for 1 hour, or until center of pie is set.

Note: Along with the pie, display a pretty basket of assorted toasts and jams. Any gourmet store carries lovely and expensive preserves. As WASP women usually don't eat much, you'll find that the toast will go fast (it absorbs the alcohol) and you'll be left with a lot of pie. If you live in Manhattan, you can always give the leftover pie to the doorman.

MOTHER'S DAY LUNCH

This is the day when WASP children thank their mothers for a fine, repressed upbringing. If it weren't for the Mums, WASPs might actually express their emotions (how indecorous) and become modern dancers or Jungian therapists, instead of even-keeled corporate lawyers and Wall Street tycoons. For it is the WASP mother who rules the household with a sterling silver fist. And it is on this day that the children can also thank their mothers for ruling so well the staff who actually raised them. We always had a luncheon on Mother's Day, spread out on antique quilts surrounded by daffodils, daisies, and tulips imported from Holland (or New Jersey).

WELLESLEY'S SPRING CHICKEN

SERVES 6

6	boneless chicken breasts
1	15-ounce bottle Italian salad dressing
1	10–12-ounce jar apricot preserves
½	package Lipton Onion Soup mix

Marinate the chicken breasts in the dressing overnight in the refrigerator.

Preheat the oven to 350° F.

Combine the preserves and soup mix, and spread over chicken in a baking pan. Cover the pan and bake for 30 minutes. Remove cover and bake for 20 minutes longer or until chicken is cooked through. Serve hot or chilled for a picnic.

POTATO AND CELERY SALAD
SERVES 10–12

4	cups cubed boiled potatoes
2	cups finely chopped celery
2	medium apples, peeled
1	15-ounce bottle French dressing

Combine the potatoes with the celery in a large bowl. Cut the apples into thin slices and add to mixture. Pour dressing over the mixture and chill until ready to serve.

BLOCK ISLAND'S SWEET SALAD
SERVES 8–10

10	large carrots, peeled	4	teaspoons grated lemon peel
1	cup currants	2	tablespoons lemon juice
1	cup chopped pecans		
1	teaspoon salt	1	cup sour cream
		1	cup mayonnaise

Grate the carrots coarsely into a large bowl. Add the remaining ingredients and toss well.

PRUNE WHIP
SERVES 8–10

This has always been a favorite in our home on Mother's Day. Sometimes we would carry it around in crystal wine glasses while we finished a croquet game. Or we would lie on our backs and lick our spoons as Mother announced with glee the list of the newest members of the social registry.

1   pound pitted prunes

1   cup granulated sugar

10   egg whites

1   tablespoon lemon juice

Cover the prunes with cold water and soak for several hours, until plumped.

Cook in same water over low heat until soft. Strain prunes well, add sugar, and cook for 5 minutes, then let cool.

Preheat the oven to 300° F.

Beat egg whites until stiff. Add cold prune mixture gradually, and then lemon juice. Pile lightly into a 1-quart buttered baking dish and bake for 20 minutes. Chill and serve cold.

BRIDAL TEA
—❖—

The bridal tea is an all-female, pre-wedding gathering of the bride's mother, sisters, aunts, grandmothers, cousins, friends, and friends of her fiancé. It's a time when the women of both families come together to get a peek at what future family gatherings will look like and to discuss the terms of the prenuptial agreement. It is a bevy of tortoise-shell barrettes and crocodile-skin loafers. You will find these women with ankles crossed and teacups in hand, discussing how lucky the bride is that her last name begins with the same letter as her fiancé's, so that the linens and towels she grew up with will still work in her new Oyster Bay home. And, of course, there is much excitement in recounting how many times Tiffany's has called with a registry update.

TEA
—❖—

1   pot Earl Grey tea (not too perfumy)

1   pot rose hips tea

1   pot Hukwa tea (if you can find it)

Always keep a small silver pitcher filled with brandy, and when someone pours a spot in her tea, always pretend not to notice.

TEA SANDWICHES

—⚜—

Bread

Butter

Mayonnaise

Watercress, a few pieces or

Cucumbers, thinly sliced or

Tomatoes, thinly sliced or

Parsley, finely chopped or

Smoked salmon

Odds and ends

Cut off bread crusts. Using a cookie cutter, cut the bread into desired shapes—triangles, hearts, money signs. Lightly butter one side of the bread and spread a touch of mayonnaise on the other. In-between, fill with one or two ingredients: the watercress, cucumbers, tomatoes, parsley, salmon, or other items.

VIRGINIA HERMITS
MAKES 12 HERMITS

—⚜—

These hermit bars are a **WASP** tradition. After a few days in the jar, however, they tend to get a bit hard.

One year my poor Grammy sat at the orchid garden party and bit into a hermit cookie, chipping her tooth! Of course, with such breeding she never even gasped and no one had any idea such an injury took place. Instead, everyone thought they had committed a horrible *faux pas* because Grammy was then silent for the rest of the afternoon. Turns out she had just been holding the damaged tooth under her tongue for safekeeping.

¼	cup butter	½	teaspoon baking soda
¼	cup lard	¼	teaspoon salt
1½	cups packed brown sugar	1	teaspoon ground cinnamon
2	eggs	¼	teaspoon. ground cloves
2	cups Vermont Guild stone-ground cornmeal	⅓	cup chopped walnuts
		⅓	cup dried currants

Preheat the oven to 350° F. Lightly grease 2 cookie sheets.

Cream the butter and lard in a large bowl. Add the brown sugar in small amounts, then add the eggs and remaining ingredients, mixing well. Dollop two teaspoonfuls each onto cookie sheets. Bake until golden brown, about 12 minutes. Cool on a wire rack.

LEMON SQUARES
MAKES 12–16 SQUARES

2	cups all-purpose flour
1	cup butter, melted
1	teaspoon vanilla extract
1	cup granulated sugar
½	cup packed brown sugar
½	cup finely chopped almonds
1	cup shredded coconut
1	egg
1	12-ounce jar lemon marmalade
½	cup confectioners' sugar

Preheat the oven to 350° F. Lightly grease a 9 x 12-inch baking pan.

In a large bowl, mix all ingredients except marmalade and confectioners' sugar. Pack three-fourths of the mixture into the bottom of the pan. Spread marmalade on top and sprinkle on remaining mixture. Bake for 40 minutes. Let cool.

Before serving, sprinkle with confectioners' sugar and cut into squares.

GRANDFATHER'S SWEET BALLS

MAKES UP TO 24 BALLS

2	cups chopped pecans
½	cup creamy peanut butter
2	cups all-purpose flour
1½	cups butter, softened
6	tablespoons granulated sugar
4	tablespoons (¼ cup) vanilla extract
½	cup confectioners' sugar

Mix all ingredients except confectioners' sugar in a large bowl. Chill for a couple of hours.

Preheat the oven to 300° F. Lightly grease a cookie sheet.

Roll tablespoons of batter in your hands into golf ball–size balls. Place on cookie sheet and bake for 30 minutes. When cool, roll in confectioners' sugar and serve.

THE WASP WEDDING

The WASP wedding is probably the biggest event of the year—that is, next to dividend payouts on RJR Nabisco stock. It is the merging of two families, two crests, two sets of silver, two summer homes, and four butlers. Nothing is paramount to perpetuating such perfectly polished lineage. A word about lineage: at the union of two WASPs, the idea is to be as closely related as possible without actually being related (in which case you're white trash and should probably be reading a different cookbook).

WASP weddings are usually celebrated at the country club or on the lawn of the family home, under a large white tent. What distinguishes a WASP wedding from any other wedding is its lack of food. Don't be surprised if you're at a wedding on Shelter Island (i.e., you're stranded without a way to the mainland and there's no Domino's) and all you see is cheese and crackers for days. I have been in these situations and found the Red Cross to be quite helpful.

CREAMED CHICKEN IN PASTRY SHELLS
SERVES 8–10

2 cups milk

2 cups heavy cream

2 10½-ounce cans cream of mushroom soup

½ cup butter, melted

1 cup grated cheddar cheese

2 10-ounce packages frozen peas, defrosted and drained

1 cup sherry

6 boneless chicken breasts, poached, drained, and chopped

½ cup chopped pimientos

Place milk, cream, soup, and butter in a large saucepan and bring to a boil. Stir in cheese until melted. Mix in peas and sherry, and simmer for 20 minutes. Add chicken and pimientos, and cook for 6 minutes. Serve in pastry shells or over toast points.

TOMATO JELLY SALAD
SERVES 8–10

2	tablespoons unflavored gelatin
¼	cup cold water
½	cup boiling water
4	cups canned tomatoes
2	tablespoons chopped onion
½	tablespoon celery seeds
2–3	whole cloves
1	teaspoon salt
1	tablespoon granulated sugar
4	teaspoons lemon juice

Soak the gelatin in cold water until soft, then dissolve in boiling water. Simmer the tomatoes, onion, celery seeds, cloves, salt, and sugar for 15 minutes. Strain through a fine strainer. Add lemon juice and gelatin mixture. Fill individual 4-cup molds that have been dipped in cold water. Chill until firm, about 6 hours.

Unmold onto plates lined with crisp lettuce and serve with that traditional **WASP** staple, mayonnaise dressing.

LEMON RICE
SERVES 4–6

- 2½ cups chicken broth
- ½ teaspoon salt
- 1 cup long-grain rice
- 3 tablespoons unsalted butter
- 2 tablespoons finely grated lemon zest (peel)

Heat the broth and salt in a large saucepan. Bring to a boil, then stir in rice. Cover and simmer for 25 minutes. Remove from heat. Stir in butter and lemon zest.

ALI'S DEVILED EGGS
SERVES 12 (WITH 2 PER PERSON)

- 12 hard-boiled eggs
- 1 6-ounce jar mayonnaise
- 1 tablespoon mustard
- ½ teaspoon curry powder

Salt and pepper

Cut the eggs lengthwise and scoop out yolks into a bowl. Mash yolks with mayonnaise, mustard, and curry powder. Add salt and pepper to taste. With a teaspoon, fill the egg white cavities with yolk mixture. They look fabulous on lace and a silver tray.

OLD BOSTON WEDDING CAKE

This cake normally serves about 30–40 people, but will serve many more because this is a turn of the century cake and most WASPs don't take to it anymore.

1	pound butter	½	teaspoon ground cloves
1	pound brown sugar	¼	cup brandy
12	eggs	2	tablespoons lemon juice
3½	cups all-purpose flour	2	pounds raisins
2	teaspoons ground cinnamon	1	pound currants
¾	teaspoon grated nutmeg	1	pound finely chopped figs
¾	teaspoon ground allspice	1	pound sugared walnuts
¾	teaspoon mace	1	pound thinly sliced citron

FROSTING

---

2   cups confectioners' sugar

1   cup fresh lemon juice

4   8-ounce packages cream cheese

¼   cup dried currants

Preheat the oven to 350° F. Butter and flour two 9 x 12-inch cake pans.

Cream the butter in a large mixing bowl. Add the brown sugar and beat thoroughly. Separate the egg yolks from the egg whites. Beat yolks until thick and lemon colored; beat whites until stiff and dry. Add yolks to butter and sugar mixture. Add flour (except ⅓ cup), spices, brandy, and lemon juice. Then add raisins, currants, figs, and nuts. Fold in egg whites. Stir the ⅓ cup flour into the citron. Pour half the batter into the pan. Spread citron mixture on top, then top with remaining batter. Bake for 1½ hours or until a cake tester inserted in center comes out clean.

Prepare the frosting.

Mix together the sugar and lemon juice. Cream the mixture with cream cheese and then stir in currants. Spread nicely over cake.

Note: This is the traditional **WASP** wedding cake; it tastes like it, and few eat it voluntarily. The important thing is to get that one traditional bite in the couple's mouths. (To get them to swallow it, give them plenty of champagne to wash it down.) Also make sure to order your boxes with the bride and groom's monogrammed initials. Every guest leaves with a box of wedding cake, a lace sack of colored candied almonds, and some Wall Street insider information.

ANNUAL FAMILY MEETING TEA

The annual family meeting used to be a time when the extended family gathered to discuss property, financial accounts, and the name of a good doctor who can declare Grandpa legally incompetent. Alas, as WASPs have slowly over the years lost much of their estates and holdings, owing to n'er-do-well offspring, the annual family meeting has become more of a de facto reunion. If you have married into such a family and are of a different background, I suggest you feign the flu or a slipped disk and stay home.

As WASPs can't cook an elaborate meal, family meetings have mercifully taken on a tealike quality.

MARY'S KNEES
SERVES 15–20

An important drink for calming nerves and provoking hearty laughs (i.e., add extra vodka).

6	cups fresh squeezed orange juice	4	cups Absolut Citron (lemon vodka)
2	cups fresh squeezed lemon juice	2	cups Grand Marnier liqueur
2	cups fresh squeezed lime juice		

Mix ingredients with plenty of ice and orange wedges.

BUNNY'S BROWNIES
MAKES 10–12 BROWNIES

1   ounce semisweet chocolate

4   ounces unsweetened baking chocolate

1   cup butter

4   eggs

2   cups granulated sugar

1   cup all-purpose flour

½   cup chopped walnuts

1   tablespoon vanilla extract

Preheat the oven to 350° F. Lightly grease a 9-inch square baking dish.

In the top of a double boiler, melt the chocolates and butter. Set aside to cool. Beat the eggs and sugar together and add to the cooled sugar mixture. Stir in the flour, nuts, and vanilla. Bake for 30 minutes or until top springs back when pushed with a finger.

BEAN'S APPLESAUCE CAKE
(Or as she called it, "Ode to Jerry" Loaf)

SERVES 6–8

It's typical for **WASP**y teenagers to rebel in some way. Usually during prep school they become Deadheads or grunge heads, but not to worry—they almost always grow up to be heads of law firms and banks. My younger sister was a "Bohemian" years ago (meaning she had a lot of bumper stickers on her Saab), and introduced us to this fabulous cake during one of the family meetings.

¾ cup packed brown sugar

1 cup thick applesauce

2 tablespoons butter, melted

1½ cups all-purpose flour

1 teaspoon vanilla extract

1 teaspoon ground cinnamon

½ teaspoon ground cloves

1 cup currants

1 teaspoon baking soda

1 shot brandy

Preheat the oven to 350° F. Lightly grease a 9 x 5-inch loaf pan.

Blend ingredients in a large bowl. Pour into loaf pan and bake for about 1 hour or until a toothpick inserted in center comes out clean.

SUMMER

OPENING–UP–THE–SUMMER–
HOUSE DINNER

CROQUET BREAKFAST

JUNE GRADUATION SUPPER

FOURTH OF JULY COOKOUT

WIMBLEDON FANCY

A HORSE TRAIL AFTERNOON

A BEACH PICNIC

VINEYARD ANTIQUE
SHOW COCKTAILS

BERMUDA RACE

LABOR DAY PICNIC

OPENING-UP-THE-SUMMER-HOUSE DINNER

Opening up the summer house can be like opening up a gift from a distant relative: you never know what you're going to get. The winter has usually been harsh (that's why the WASPs are in Hobe Sound), causing paint to peel, furniture to wear out, and stone walls to age. But don't fret, they say it's the most tortured grapes that make the finest vintages. The duress your summer home suffers in the off months gives all your WASP possessions that priceless and impossible-to-imitate Ralph Lauren patina.

After traveling so far on the ferry or in the Volvo station wagon, sponging off the furniture, and washing the Laura Ashley sheets, WASPs reward themselves with their first lobsters (or Lobby's, as they're called) of summer.

STEAMED LOBSTERS
SERVES 8

8   1½-pound Maine lobsters (or
    lobsters from whatever island
    you're on; I prefer Maine)

1   pound unsalted butter, melted

Pinch of sea salt

3   lemons, squeezed for juice

Fill a large steel lobster pot and steamer halfway with water or Heineken (it works) and bring to a boil. Place the lobsters in the steamer on top and cover with lid. Steam for 20 minutes or until the lobsters are bright red.

Crack the claws with a nut or lobster cracker (or if there is a judge in the family, use his silver gavel). Serve with melted butter flavored with a bit of sea salt and lemon juice.

GREEN LEAF SALAD
SERVES 8

1   head Boston or butter lettuce

1   bunch red oak leaf lettuce

½   15-ounce bottle Newman's Own
    Salad Dressing

Wash and dry the lettuces. Combine in a large wooden salad bowl. Pour dressing on top and toss gingerly.

ICE CREAM MEDLEY

1   pint Ben & Jerry's Cherry Garcia ice cream

1   pint Ben & Jerry's Mint Oreo Cookie ice cream

1   pint Ben & Jerry's Chunky Monkey ice cream

Take a bunch of the family's silver spoons and the ice cream, and head out to the lawn. With large Pierre Deux pillows for your heads, lie back and look at the Big Dipper, eat the ice cream, and dream about who will have the biggest schooner that summer.

CROQUET
BREAKFAST

WASPs love croquet because they get to dress up and drink, and it's less strenuous than exercising a stock option. And what better to do with those perfectly manicured lawns? WASPs are fascinated by croquet because it's the only sport you can play while, quite literally, holding a drink in your hand (in fact, the polo mallet can actually steady you!). It always amazed me that, after seven Bloody Marys, my great uncle was still able to send balls flying off the property (taking a few dachshunds with them) and into the sand dunes. If you happen to be the receiver of such a hit, you may as well join the rest of the family on the porch for grapefruit mimosas and breakfast.

WALKER'S BLUEBERRY MUFFINS

MAKES 12 MUFFINS

1½ cups milk

3   cups all-purpose flour

2   eggs

1¼ cups butter

1   tablespoon baking powder

½   teaspoon baking soda

Pinch of salt

1½ cups granulated sugar

2   cups blueberries

Preheat the oven to 350° F. Lightly butter 2 muffin tins.

Combine all the ingredients except the blueberries in a large bowl. Gently fold in the blueberries as not to crush them. Spoon the batter into the muffin tins almost to the top. Bake until lightly browned, about 25 minutes. Cool briefly on a wire rack.

AUNT LULU'S FRUIT SALAD
SERVES 6–8

This salad was a family tradition on sticky summer mornings. Aunt Lulu experimented with different fruits, but this turned out to be the only combination that even worked somewhat. Unfortunately, she eventually lost her marbles and—oddly—the only thing she even remembered about her life was this recipe.

1   15-ounce can crushed pineapple

1   envelope peach-flavored gelatin

2   cups buttermilk

1   12-ounce container Cool Whip topping

1   15-ounce can apricot halves, pitted and drained

In a large saucepan, heat the pineapple with its juice until it boils. Dissolve gelatin in the pineapple and let cool. Add the buttermilk and fold in the Cool Whip. Pour into a 6-cup mold and chill for 24 hours. Adorn the top with the apricots.

FEATHERED EGG NEST
SERVES 8–10

12	slices white bread
2	cups grated cheddar cheese
1½	pounds cooked pork sausage, crumbled
8	eggs
1¾	cups milk
1	teaspoon mustard
1	teaspoon pepper

Salt, to taste

Preheat the oven to 350° F. Butter a large, rectangular glass baking dish.

Place the bread slices in the bottom of the dish; sprinkle cheese and sausage evenly over bread. Mix the rest of the ingredients in a bowl and pour over the bread. Bake for 40 minutes, or until eggs are set.

JUNE GRADUATION SUPPER

Nothing makes WASP parents happier than seeing their money not go to waste, which is why they don't buy Italian cars or attend couture shows. On graduation day, they are chomping at the bit for junior to join the firm (a job he has practically secured since birth). And now that their daughter has received her master's in art history, she's ready to marry well and volunteer at the Met. With all this to celebrate, make sure there is always plenty of champagne and toasts at the graduation supper. And take note: any heirlooms given that day should be placed immediately in the bank vault. My sister made the mistake of drinking too much bubbly and tried to swallow her graduation gift, our great-grandmother's diamond bracelet.

WATCH HILL FLOUNDER WHEELS
SERVES 8–10

2 cups crushed Ritz Crackers

Salt, to taste

1½ cups grated Parmesan cheese

6 tablespoons chopped onion

1 cup butter

¼ cup dry white wine

3 tablespoons lemon juice

3 pounds flounder fillets

Preheat the oven to 375° F.

Mix crackers, salt, Parmesan, and onion in a bowl. Melt the butter, add the wine and lemon juice, then stir into the cracker mixture. Place 2 tablespoons of the mixture on the broad end of each flounder fillet, roll up fillet (like rolling up a sleeping bag), and secure with a toothpick. Place in a lightly greased baking dish and bake for 30 minutes, or until fish flakes.

Note: When this recipe seems too difficult, WASPs have been known to just take a whole fish, cover it in gin, and bake it. I know if I were a fish, that's how I'd want to go.

CREAMED SPINACH PUREE
SERVES 8–10

3 tablespoons butter

2 tablespoons all-purpose flour

1 teaspoon salt

1½ cups milk

4 cups cooked, chopped spinach

Melt the butter in saucepan. Blend in the flour, salt, and milk, and stir constantly over low heat until the mixture has a thick consistency. In a food processor, puree the mixture with the chopped spinach.

HOBART MASHED POTATOES
SERVES 8–10

3   pounds white potatoes, peeled

1   cup unsalted butter

1   8-ounce package cream cheese

½   cup heavy cream

Salt and pepper, to taste

Boil the potatoes for 30 minutes or until soft. Drain and mash them with the butter, cream cheese, cream, salt, and pepper. Whip until smooth.

BOSTON CAKE
SERVES 15–20

⅔   cup butter

2   cups granulated sugar

4   eggs, lightly beaten

1   cup milk

3½   cups all-purpose flour

5   teaspoons baking powder

ORANGE FROSTING

— ✤ —

4	orange rinds, grated
2	teaspoons brandy
¼	cup orange juice
2	tablespoons lemon juice
1	8-ounce package cream cheese

Confectioners' sugar, enough to thicken

Preheat the oven to 350° F. Lightly butter two 9 x 5-inch loaf pans.

Cream the butter in a large mixing bowl. Add the sugar, eggs, and milk. Sift together the flour and baking powder, then add gradually to egg mixture. Pour batter equally into loaf pans. Bake for 25 minutes, or until golden brown. Let cool on wire racks.

Prepare frosting.

Add grated rind to brandy and fruit juices, then let stand for 30 minutes. Strain and add cream cheese. Stir in confectioners' sugar until thick, frosting consistency. Place one loaf on top of the other and frost cooled cakes. Use bits of orange rind to creatively spell Summa cum Laude on top of cakes.

FOURTH OF JULY COOKOUT

On the Fourth of July you'll find WASPs huddled, in their American-flag knit sweaters, up and down the Eastern Seaboard, watching fireworks from private beaches such as Wingersheik. Many have cookouts in the sand or on their sailboats. I don't recommend grilling on the boat, because of the likelihood of an accident; as alluring as inheritance money is, collecting from tragedy is always bittersweet.

By the way, WASPs spend so much money on Burberry coats, shirts custom tailored on Bond Street, and Range Rovers that it's a wonder why they ever wanted their independence from England!

MEREDITH FAMILY'S STEAMED CLAMS

SERVES 15–20

You can always find the tow-headed Meredith Family in cut off khakis and faded navy turtlenecks, with their flat bottoms up in the air, digging through the sand for the earth's crown jewels—steamer clams. You can see them sifting around at the crack of dawn, almost lost in the Oak Bluffs mist, yelling "Over here, Cozzie. They're fat ones!" And if you're lucky enough to receive an invitation for dinner that week, you can rest assured it will be delicious. This WASP family knows how to cook a clam.

> 10 pounds steamer clams
>
> 2 pounds unsalted butter, melted
>
> Salt, to taste
>
> 2 lemons, squeezed for juice

Wash and scrub the clams very well under cold water. Place the clams in 3 to 4 inches of boiling water in a steamer kettle and close the lid. Steam until the clams open.

Serve with bowls of salted melted butter and lemon juice for dipping. Also, a bowl of plain hot water is good for rinsing off sand from the clams.

FIRE ROASTED CORN
SERVES 12

—✤—

12   ears white corn

1   cup salted butter

Salt

Have a charcoal or wood fire ready, with ash-covered coals.

Shuck and clean the corn. Spread butter and salt on each ear, then roll it up in foil so that the ear is completely covered. Place on the embers for about 10 minutes. The corn may get a little burnt, but it is tasty.

STEAMED RED POTATOES
SERVES 15–20

—✤—

10   pounds red potatoes

1   pound butter, melted

Salt, to taste

Chopped parsley

Steam the red potatoes with the clams if the pot is big enough. Or while everyone is chomping down the clams, use the pot to steam the potatoes.

In 4 inches of liquid, steam the potatoes for 15–20 minutes with the pot covered. When done, drain and drizzle with butter. Add salt and sprinkle with parsley.

WATERMELON BASKET
SERVES 18–20

The watermelon basket is a must at summer WASP functions, for two important reasons: it contains alcohol and it looks beautiful! And picking the blueberries is always something for the children to do, especially if badminton gets boring.

1	whole watermelon
4	baskets blueberries
½	quart chilled vodka
¼	cup fresh lemon juice

Don't drink before executing this task! Cut the watermelon into a basket shape by cutting a large triangular wedge in either side of the melon. Scoop out the watermelon meat with a melon baller. Add the watermelon balls to the blueberries and mix. Combine the vodka and lemon juice and add to the mixture. Place the fruit mixture in the watermelon basket. Garnish with fresh white roses.

WIMBLEDON FANCY

WASPs have been quite taken with strawberries and cream ever since it was introduced as the signature refreshment at Wimbledon, just as they were with the shirt worn at this tournament by the late French tennis star René Lacoste. As this is not a complicated recipe, most WASP women actually attempt to make it as their cook (masking giggles) observes.

This dessert is best served in individual silver bowls. If the bowls are being polished and Tiffany's is closed, a second choice is your grandmother's Herend wedding china soup bowls. A note to non-WASPs: When you are served these bowls full of warm water and lemon, it is not a soup. It is a finger-dipping bowl with which to clean your fingers. WASP cooking is known to be so tasteless that guests have often sipped this instead and thought it the star dish of the dinner.

STRAWBERRIES AND CREAM
SERVES 8–10

Enjoy this while watching the Wimbledon finals in your private box, or on the television at the club.

2	quarts whole strawberries (or wild, if available)
2	pints heavy cream
2	tablespoons confectioners' sugar per helping
1	16-ounce box Cadbury Chocolate Fingers

Wash and cut the hulls off all the strawberries. Place in serving bowls. Whip the cream until thick but still runny. Drape the cream over the strawberries and sprinkle with sugar. The chocolate fingers are the decorative finale—place one to the side of each bowl.

A HORSE TRAIL AFTERNOON

The Connecticut and New Hampshire WASPs like to spend their summer afternoons exploring their grounds on horseback, many pleasantly surprised at the full expanse of their property. Besides their love for horses, WASPs relish an excuse to get bedecked from head to toe in Ralph Lauren wear—khaki jodhpurs (the classy answer to Spandex), tweed jackets, floral scarves, and burgundy calf-skin gloves.

WHITE GRAPE PUNCH
SERVES 15–20

Such exercise makes for a big thirst, but don't give any to the horses or you'll be walking home.

1	quart white grape juice	2	tablespoons lemon juice
½	cup granulated sugar	2	tablespoons lime juice
½	bottle chardonnay (such as Pouilley-Fuissé)	1	14-ounce bottle club soda

Mix all the ingredients and chill well. When ready, add ice cubes or an ice ring to keep cool on the trail.

CHICKEN WALNUT SALAD

SERVES 6–8

The curry powder is so exotic—it's for the daring and well-traveled WASP.

    4   large boneless chicken breasts

    1   cup walnuts

    2   dozen red grapes

    1   cup chopped celery

Salt and pepper

    2   teaspoons curry powder

    1   cup mayonnaise

Poach the chicken breasts and cut into bite-size pieces. Add the walnuts, grapes, celery, salt, pepper, and curry powder; mix well. Stir in the mayonnaise. Chill and serve.

HAYRIDE COOKIES

MAKES 24 COOKIES

1	cup butter
1	cup packed brown sugar
1	cup granulated sugar
2	eggs
3	teaspoons vanilla extract
2	cups all-purpose flour
2	teaspoons baking soda
1½	cups chocolate chips
1	cup Raisinettes

Preheat the oven to 350° F. Lightly grease 2 cookie sheets.

Cream the butter in a large mixing bowl. Add the sugars, eggs, and vanilla. Gradually stir in the flour and baking soda. Add the chocolate chips and Raisinettes. Place by teaspoonfuls on cookie sheets and bake for 15 minutes. Cool on a wire rack.

A BEACH PICNIC
— ❧ —

Before the *WASP* children head out to Chase
Tennis Camp and Outward Bound, the family
likes to secure precious time together on such private beaches as Nantucket and Martha's
Vineyard. The beach is always strewn with gold-
en Labs jumping for Frisbees, boys playing Nerf
lacrosse, and girls working on their deep tans, all
the better to set off their white oxford shirts.
These beaches are a favorite *WASP* hangout;
they are that rare island paradise where the natives
look like *WASP*s and even speak their language.
Summer residents can always be spotted by their
Trinity boxers and Black Dog T-shirts.

Note: Every *WASP* must have a picnic basket that's at least sixty years old. If you don't have
one, buy a new basket and bury it in the ground
for a year.

MUFFIE'S FAMOUS SANDWICH

MAKES 30–40 PETITE SANDWICHES

8   vine-ripened tomatoes

8   vine-ripened yellow tomatoes

Homemade bread, sliced (Pepperidge Farm is fine)

1   12-ounce jar mayonnaise

Cut the tomatoes as thin as possible. Arrange the slices on half the bread slices. Take 1 tablespoon of mayonnaise and put it in the middle. Press the other slice of bread on top. Cut off the crust and cut into 4 triangles.

CELERY STICKS

1   bunch celery, trimmed and cut into 4-inch pieces

1   16-ounce package cream cheese

Freshly ground pepper

Marigold petals from 1 dozen flowers

Fill the grooves of the celery stalks with cream cheese. With a knife, smooth the tops. Sprinkle with pepper. Add marigold petals for a festive touch.

WASPs usually pick up everything else for a picnic at the general store—Snapple Ice Tea, potato chips, and Cow Patties (gourmet cookies).

VINEYARD ANTIQUE SHOW COCKTAILS

For *WASPs* it's always fun to collect more heirlooms, even if they're someone else's. It's also exciting for *WASPs* to see that all the chipped tea trays and broken grandfather clocks that have been lying around their homes for years actually are worth staggering sums of money.

As children we used to play a game at the antique shows. We had to find something monogrammed, like an ice bucket or a cigarette case, that matched our initials. Unfortunately, I ran into a bit of trouble when, so desperately wanting to win, I carved my initials onto the top of a very expensive Queen Anne dining room table.

After an afternoon of hobnobbing with famous female authors and New York Times columnists on vacation, *WASPs* usually gather at someone's home and share a drink (and laugh at the poor fool who spent too much on a clearly faux nineteenth-century watercolor).

CHIPPENDALE COCKTAIL
MAKES 2–4 DRINKS
(DEPENDING ON THE TAKE)

1	cup whiskey
1	cup lemonade
6	ice cubes
1	lemon, sliced

Combine all ingredients in a cocktail shaker and shake well. Pour into flute glasses, adding a lemon wedge to each one.

JEFFEREY'S CRAB DIP
SERVES 8–10

¾	cup mayonnaise
¾	cup sour cream
2	lemons, squeezed for juice
3	pinches cracked peppercorns
2	cups fresh lump bluefin crabmeat
Triscuit crackers	

Blend the mayonnaise and sour cream together. Add the lemon juice and peppercorns. Slowly stir in crab. Serve with Triscuits.

MUMMY'S VEGETABLE PLATE
— ⚜ —

My mother always uses this dip for informal cock-tail gatherings or black-tie fund-raisers.

1	cup mayonnaise	Carrots
2	tablespoons curry powder	Celery sticks
		Radishes
1	teaspoon Worcestershire sauce	Cauliflower spears
		Green beans
Squirt of lemon juice		Asparagus
Cherry tomatoes		Scallions

Blend the mayonnaise, curry powder, Worcestershire, and lemon juice in a bowl. Chill.

Serve the dip chilled, surrounded by groups of raw vegetables, mixing them together by color.

BERMUDA RACE

—✦—

Every summer is the sailboat race from Newport, Rhode Island, to Bermuda—the Island. It's a great excuse not only to dust off the yachtsmanship you learned at Deerfield Academy but to check in on your offshore accounts. WASPs like to host their own cocktail parties on their boats or at the yacht club, then fly to Bermuda a few days before the boats finish to get a tan, buy cashmere sweaters from Trimingham's, and be part of the welcoming committee with silver chalices full of champagne. You'll see this same group at the Edgartown Regatta, as well. In Newport, WASPs line the decks with their black Labradors, Patagonia fleece jackets, and J. Crew shorts slurping Newport's infamous clam chowder.

NEWPORT CLAM CHOWDER
SERVES 20–30

—◈—

I don't recommend this for the impending captain and crew in case of rocky weather and large swells—you get my point!

2	quarts fresh steamer clams
1	cube (2½ inches) salt pork
2	onions, sliced
2	quarts cubed potatoes
2	tablespoons salt
1	tablespoon pepper
½	cup all-purpose flour
2½	cups boiling water
2	quarts milk, scalded
½	cup butter

Oyster crackers
Cracked peppercorns

Clean the clams thoroughly under cold water. In a large pan, put the clams in about 1 cup of water and bring to a boil, then remove from heat and strain. Chop clams into quarters. Cut salt pork into small pieces and sauté in pan; add onion and cook for 5 minutes. Drain and place potatoes and clams in a large stew pot. Sprinkle with salt and pepper, then dredge with flour. Add boiling water and cook for 10 minutes. Add milk, clams, and butter and cook for 20 minutes. Sprinkle crackers and cracked peppercorns on top. Serve with chilled Molsons.

LABOR DAY PICNIC

End-of-summer picnics are always hard because they are the big send-off to all the old and new summer friends. On the other hand, by Labor Day, the gossip is exhausted and the love affairs are unwinding, so perhaps it is best we say good-bye. Many a Labor Day I spent hidden in the dunes, with binoculars in hand, watching my sister say good-bye to the summer tennis pro or the freckled boy heading off to Exeter Academy that fall. The Labor Day picnic is also the final meal to enjoy the wealth of summer delights.

LOBSTER ROLLS
MAKES 12 ROLLS

— ✦ —

You must book-end the summer with lobster.

> 12   hot dog rolls
> Meat of 6 cooked lobsters, shredded
> 1   8-ounce jar mayonnaise
> 1   lemon, squeezed for juice

Lightly toast the hot dog rolls. In a medium bowl, combine the shredded lobster meat, mayonnaise, and lemon juice. Stir until well mixed. With an ice cream scooper, scoop the lobster meat into each hot dog bun. Be sure to serve with plenty of napkins.

Note: Always be sure to buy the lobster fresh from the local fish market. It is expensive to set your own traps, and if you've had too many cocktails and pick up someone else's trap, you're likely to get hurt (more importantly—shot!). WASPs are quite serious about their "summer pheasants."

SISSY'S COLESLAW
SERVES 10–12

½   head green cabbage

½   head red cabbage

1   cup milk

2   tablespoons all-purpose flour

1   teaspoon mustard

¼   cup red wine vinegar

2   teaspoons granulated sugar

2   teaspoons salt

2   egg yolks

Shred the cabbage the same way you do long distance phone bills when you're having an affair. Place in a large salad bowl.

Whisk together the remaining ingredients in a bowl and drizzle over shredded cabbage. Mix well and serve.

In addition, my mother also brought to the picnic a big basket of cherry tomatoes from our garden. We would simply dip the tomatoes in a bowl of salt—not just salt, but salt Daddy would buy in Paris at Fauchon every year—and plop it in our mouths. They were almost like eating candy.

KIKI'S CUPCAKES
MAKES APPROXIMATELY 24 CUPCAKES
—⚜—

Kiki's specialty was not only baking cupcakes and marrying well but devising a special treat by hiding a dime in the batter. Anyone who bit into the cupcake with the coin—and didn't choke—received a one-dollar bill as the prize. (Those that did choke received a somewhat larger settlement.) Note: Don't try this at home.

⅔	cup butter	3½	cups all-purpose flour
2	cups granulated sugar	½	teaspoon mace
4	eggs	1	tablespoon baking powder
1	cup milk		

BILLOWY CLOUD FROSTING
—⚜—

6	tablespoons butter
1	pound box confectioners' sugar
½	cup light cream
2	teaspoons vanilla extract

Preheat the oven to 350° F. Lightly grease muffin tins or use paper liners.

Mix the butter, sugar, eggs, and milk in a large

bowl. Slowly add the flour, mace, and baking powder. Stir until creamy. Pour batter into cupcake cups
and bake until golden brown on top. Cool on a wire
rack.

Prepare the frosting.

Cream the butter; add the sugar and blend well.
Beat in the cream and the vanilla. Spread with a
butter knife atop the cupcakes.

Autumn

Prep School Send-Off

Head-of-the-Charles Picnic

Harvard-Yale Game
Tailgate Party

A Middleburg Foxhunt

Harvard Punching
Party Lunch

A Racquetball Brunch

PREP SCHOOL
SEND-OFF

Dreaded are the early days of September when the young WASPs, dressed in plaid with Brooks Brothers jackets are shipped away for higher learning to St. Paul's or Andover. Nevertheless, for some reason, to be sent away at an age when you've barely stopped breast-feeding, have not even begun puberty, and still suck your thumb is considered a great WASP honor.

When I was dropped off at an all-girls boarding school, it took my parents three hours to pry my arms off the bumper of their Volvo station wagon. And as you study the classics, get hit in the head with lacrosse sticks, and debate club your way through a dark winter of influenza, it's always great excitement to receive some homemade goodies. The note always says "Love, Mom" or "Mother" or "Muzzie," dictated but not read, and even though you know it's the cook who made them, you're grateful.

INEZ'S COOKIES

MAKES APPROXIMATELY 20–30 COOKIES

—✦—

1¼ cups butter

1 cup packed light brown sugar

1 cup granulated sugar

2 eggs

1 tablespoon vanilla extract

2 cups all-purpose flour

1 teaspoon baking soda

1 teaspoon salt

1½ cups chocolate chips

1 cup chopped walnuts (optional)

Preheat the oven to 350° F. Lightly grease cookie sheets.

Cream the butter with the sugars. Add the eggs and vanilla, and mix well. Stir in all other ingredients. Drop by tablespoonfuls onto cookie sheets and bake for 15 minutes. Cool on a wire rack.

HEAD-OF-THE-CHARLES PICNIC

Every October, about 100,000 WASPs converge in Boston to watch the crew races of prep school and college shells glide up and down the Charles River. And it's a lot more fun to be drunk when the whole town is. Some say the races are completely boring, but you do get to mingle with attractive WASPs from Colby, Bates, and Princeton. Unfortunately, there is so much socializing and networking that little attention is paid to the poor souls freezing out there on the river or crashing into the bridge.

WHISKEY SOURS
MAKES 1 DRINK

¼   cup lemon juice

1   teaspoon granulated sugar

4   ounces (½ cup) whiskey

Cracked ice

1   maraschino cherry

Shake the lemon juice, sugar, and whiskey well with the cracked ice. Strain into an old-fashioned glass and garnish with a cherry.

TROUT'S SAUSAGE PIE
SERVES 8–10

This is also served at the Henley crew races (not Don Henley) at Henley-on-Thames, England, if you need to be more formal (i.e., snotty).

> Dough for 2 9-inch pie crusts
> 1½ pounds Italian sausage
> 1 10-ounce package frozen spinach, thawed and drained
> 1 cup ricotta cheese
> 1 12-ounce package mozzarella cheese, grated
> 1 8-ounce can mushrooms
> 6 eggs
> Salt, to taste

Preheat the oven to 350° F.

Pat the dough for 1 pie crust into a 9-inch pie pan. Crumble in the sausage, spinach, cheeses, and mushrooms. Beat the eggs and salt and pour over the filling. Place the second crust on top and cut small slits. Bake for 40 minutes, or until crust is nicely browned. Serve hot.

HARVARD-YALE GAME TAILGATE PARTY

—◆—

Only perhaps on Wall Street can you see more WASP men converge upon each other with such unbridled hostility than at the Harvard-Yale football game. You'll recognize the WASP men in the stands by their beaver coats, Harvard or Yale caps, and arms around some blond Elizabeth or Charlotte, who looks utterly bored.

There are always competing tailgate parties on this day. The real competition is not who's scoring a touchdown, but who's got the best martini—"a soft drink turneth away company." The cocktail fest is served right out of the back of the Jeep Wagoneer on an L.L. Bean blanket, with silver martini shakers monogrammed with Poppy's graduating year. Don't let the real linen napkins and fine silver fool you, though. The liquor is always cheap and in extra-large gallon sizes because it's quantity, not quality, that scores points at this event.

A Dry Martini à la Noel Coward

Makes 2–3 drinks

The old joke goes: how many **WASP**s does it take to change a lightbulb? Two. One to screw it in and the other to make the martinis.

Now, about making those martinis:

6	tablespoons vermouth
6	ice cubes
¾	cup dry gin
6	cocktail olives

Pour the vermouth over ice cubes in a glass; let stand 2 minutes. Pour vermouth out, leaving a film around the ice cubes. Pour in gin and gently stir. Strain liquid into martini glasses and daintily drop in olives.

Clam Dip and Chips

In case you forgot your silver tray, fear not. New Haven and Boston are loaded with antique stores.

1   7-ounce can minced clams, drained

1   8-ounce package cream cheese

5   tablespoons mayonnaise

2   tablespoons lemon juice

½   cup grated onion

1   teaspoon horseradish

1   teaspoon Worcestershire sauce

Mix all ingredients in a large bowl. Serve on a silver tray with potato chips.

SIRLOIN BITES
MAKES 48 SMALL SANDWICHES

Mayonnaise

1   loaf thinly sliced white bread

Watercress

1   12-ounce medium-rare sirloin steak, very thinly sliced

Salt and pepper, to taste

Smear mayonnaise on one side of each bread slice. Add a sprig of watercress and slices of beef until they cover the surface of the bread. Add salt and pepper to taste. Place other slice of bread on top. Cut off crusts and quarter.

A MIDDLEBURG FOXHUNT

Whereas to the ordinary citizen a foxhunt might refer to trolling for a suitable mate, to the WASP a foxhunt means exactly that—hunting for foxes. (In WASP parlance, searching for a suitable mate is known as buying a BMW.) Foxhunting is really the WASP's tour de force, which is why it's always prominently displayed in oil paintings, on needlepoint pillows, on toilet seat covers, and everywhere else one might look in a WASP estate. In the autumn mornings, you can hear the horn and the yelping of the hounds as they jump stone fences and parade through your field. (Not a good day to wear the fox fur stoll.)

MIDDLEBURG'S MULLED CIDER

SERVES APPROXIMATELY 50

Most men will flock to their whiskey, but here's a choice for those who want something to sip with food.

1   gallon apple cider

8   cinnamon sticks

1   cup granulated sugar

10 whole cloves

2   bottles red Burgundy wine

Heat all ingredients (except the wine) to a boil, then remove from heat. Add wine and serve immediately.

KATIE'S HUNT SPREAD
SERVES 15–20

3   cups ground country ham

1   8-ounce package cream cheese

½   cup chopped pecans

Place the ingredients in a food processor and blend until smooth. Serve with stone-ground wheat crackers.

OYSTER PUFFS
SERVES 40

2	teaspoons minced onion	1	pound oysters, drained and chopped
2	teaspoons onion juice	½	cup butter
1	8-ounce package cream cheese	40	bread rounds
2	teaspoons prepared horseradish		

In a bowl, stir together the onion and onion juice, cream cheese, and horseradish. Add the oysters. Melt the butter in a frying pan and sauté the bread rounds until golden brown. Remove from pan and place on a baking sheet. Spread oyster mixture on each round and broil for 2 minutes.

DEVON'S DELIGHTS
SERVES 40

1	box Triscuit crackers
3	pounds smoked bacon, sliced

Around each cracker, wrap a strip of bacon. Set them on a buttered cooking sheet and broil for 5 minutes or until bacon is cooked.

HARVARD PUNCHING PARTY LUNCH

The Harvard punching party is an old WASP club initiation ritual wherein a select few freshmen and sophomores receive a note under their dorm room door, inviting them to play football at the prestigious Hunnewell Estate. This is to determine who will be admitted into such Ivy League secret societies as the Porcelian Club. In their khakis and cashmere turtlenecks, doing their finest impression of a J. Crew catalog come to life, WASP youths roll around and tackle each other amid the changing leaves. You almost expect Ryan O'Neal and Ali McGraw to come running in and join.

WHITFORD'S CREAMED BEEF

SERVES 15–20

4	tablespoon butter	½	cup sherry
1	cup heavy cream	1	10-oz. package frozen peas, defrosted and drained
1	cup milk		
1	10½-ounce can cream of mushroom soup	3	cups chipped beef
½	cup grated cheddar cheese		Toast points

In a large saucepan, melt the butter over medium heat. Add the cream, milk, and mushroom soup and bring to a boil. Add the cheese and stir until melted. Add the sherry and peas, then simmer for 15 minutes. Add the chipped beef and simmer for 5 more minutes. Pour over toast points and serve.

JANE'S TOMATO PUDDING
SERVES APPROXIMATELY 20

—❧—

8	cups canned tomatoes, peeled and drained
1½	cups seasoned croutons
1½	cups granulated sugar
½	cup butter, melted

Preheat the oven to 350° F.

Mix ingredients in a large bowl and pour into a casserole dish. Bake for 1 hour, or until bubbly.

BAKED CUSTARD
SERVES 12–15

—❧—

WASPs never bothered to give this a more exciting name.

6	softly beaten eggs
½	cup granulated sugar
½	teaspoon salt
2	teaspoons vanilla extract
4	cups scalded milk

Preheat the oven to 325° F.

Combine the eggs, sugar, and salt in a large mixing bowl. Stir in the vanilla and cooled milk. Pour into a 1-quart casserole dish. Set the dish on a shallow pan filled with two inches of hot water. Bake for 1 hour.

A RACQUETBALL BRUNCH

Clubsmanship is a life-long pursuit of all WASPs. In fact, there is an old WASP saying, to paraphrase Groucho Marx, "I'd never want to be a member of a club that would have you as a member."

Racquetball, squash, and paddle tennis are the ultimate WASP sports because they're a good way to work the old-boy network while getting a little cardiovascular exercise as a bonus. Not only that, but it's the perfect excuse to join an exclusive racquetball club (yet another WASP watering hole).

Sunday brunch always follows a strenuous squash game to further aid in getting rid of a hangover, exchanging gossip about the party the night before (where do you think Liz Smith gets her column), and most important, having an excuse to drink before noon.

BOOTSY'S MIMOSAS
MAKES 50–60 DRINKS

2   quarts fresh grapefruit juice

2   quarts cranberry juice

1   bottle extra-dry champagne, chilled

1   cup cold vodka

Combine the grapefruit and cranberry juices and chill. Before serving, pour in the chilled champagne and vodka to mix.

BLOODIES
MAKES 1 DRINK

½   cup fresh tomato juice

¾   cup chilled vodka

2   tablespoons lemon juice

Pinch of pepper

Pinch of celery salt

1   tablespoon lime juice

6   drops Tabasco sauce

8   drops Worcestershire sauce

Blend together all ingredients and pour over ice. Add a celery stick, lemon wedge, and more vodka.

"Cut up a true **WASP** and he doesn't bleed blood, he bleeds Bloody Mary."

J. J.'s Eggs
SERVES 8–10

Unless you're at a restaurant, in which case all the **WASP**s order eggs Benedict.

8	eggs
1	cup grated cheddar cheese
2	tomatoes, finely diced
3	scallions, finely chopped

Pinch of salt
Pinch of pepper
Dash of Tabasco sauce

Whip all ingredients together in a large bowl. Heat a large pan, add egg mixture, and cool, stirring constantly until set. Don't forget to overcook!

WINTER

DEBUTANTE BALL COCKTAILS

VAIL WEEKEND

CARIBBEAN COCKTAILS

BOXING DAY LUNCH

BLESSING OF THE HOUNDS

A WASP FUNERAL SUPPER

DEBUTANTE BALL COCKTAILS

—◆—

A young woman's debutante ball is as important—if not more important—than her wedding, for it is the marrying of an aristocratic girl to society, and no one could ask for a better first husband! The ball is also referred to as the "coming-out" party, which is not by way of the closet, but out of obscurity and into society's "A list."

These elegant debutanes, in their Bergdorf white gowns and long white gloves, are presented by their fathers. After the brief ceremony, they are toasted as the paragons of fine breeding, good taste, and decorum. They then spend the rest of the evening getting drunk, smoking cigarettes, and giving new meaning to the term "fine breeding."

At this event no one really eats because everyone is too busy table hopping. As one might guess after tasting them, the hors d'oeuvres really serve more as props rather than as actual nourishment. Nevertheless, hors d'oeuvres perform a vital function since the left hand is holding a drink and the right hand needs something to do.

CREAM PUFFS
MAKES 12 PUFFS

1   7-ounce can minced clams, drained

1   8-ounce package cream cheese

½   teaspoon salt

4   teaspoons lemon juice

2   tablespoons grated onion

2   tablespoons Worcestershire sauce

1   egg white, stiffly beaten

Toast rounds

Preheat the oven to 450° F.

Mix all ingredients except the toast in a large bowl. Place on toast rounds and bake for 3 minutes.

NUMMIES

The fancy version of nummies is fresh figs filled with gorgonzola cheese. The WASP version is dried apricots filled with Boursin cheese.

SALMON MOUSSE AND TOASTS
SERVES 12–15

Salmon mousse is to WASPs what matzo ball soup is to Jews. It has become the traditional dish that WASPs, as a group, are identified with.

1   1-pound can fancy salmon, drained

1   envelope unflavored gelatin

½   cup boiling water

¼   cup lemon juice

1   small onion, chopped

¾   cup mayonnaise

½   pint heavy cream

Toast points

Place the salmon into a large bowl (make sure the bones are removed). In another bowl, add the water to the gelatin and let it soften.

Add the lemon juice and onion to the salmon. Mix in the gelatin and mayonnaise; blend well. Slowly add the cream. Pour the mixture into an oiled 6–8-cup fish mold and chill until firm, several hours. Serve with toast points.

MICHELLE'S ARTICHOKE DIP

SERVES 20–25

2   8-ounce cans artichoke hearts

2   cups mayonnaise

½   cup chopped onion

2¼   cups grated Parmesan cheese

2   tablespoons Worcestershire sauce

¼   teaspoon pepper

¼   cup grated Monterey Jack cheese

Preheat the oven to 350° F.

Combine all ingredients except the Monterey Jack. Place in a glass baking dish, and sprinkle cheese on top. Bake for 25 minutes or until lightly browned. Serve with little round toasts.

You'll find WASPs enjoy artichoke dip, but not artichokes themselves. Artichokes have often been referred to by WASPs as "vegetables you rub on your teeth."

VAIL WEEKEND

We were told as children that the three sports at which a WASP must be proficient are skiing, tennis, and mixing cocktails. You'll find many WASPs during Christmas vacation in such places as Vail, Aspen, and Sugarbush, on the chairlift sipping hot toddies. I remember our ski lodge at Vail because, at two years old, I was pushed down the mountain on plastic red skis to ensure my fine athleticism down the road. Luckily, fractured jaws heal well and the ensuing lockjaw only helped me as a WASP.

OUR FAMILY'S EGGNOG
SERVES 6–8

6	eggs, separated
2	cups granulated sugar
¾	cup rum
3	cups bourbon whiskey
2½	cups heavy cream
2½	cups milk
Grated nutmeg	

Beat the egg yolks well in a bowl. In another bowl, beat the egg whites until stiff, then fold in the sugar. Fold the yolks into the whites and stir. Add the rum, bourbon, cream, and milk; beat well. Pour into a crystal punch bowl and sprinkle nutmeg on top.

CHEESE FONDUE

This was always a big hit in the 1970s, and you'll find it is still a winter WASP must! Ask any WASP mother or her housekeeper, and you're sure to find a fondue set somewhere in the pantry.

To most people, fondue is an hors d'oeuvre; to WASPs it's dinner.

1 pound sharp cheddar cheese, grated

1 cup beer (Heineken, Molson)

2 tablespoons mustard

Pinch of salt

1 loaf white bread, cubed

Melt the cheese, beer, mustard, and salt in a fondue pot. Heat slowly and stir frequently until well blended. Stick a cube of white bread at the end of a fondue fork and dip into melted sauce. (Keep the fondue warm over a small fondue flame.)

CARIBBEAN COCKTAILS

During Christmas vacation, if you don't see WASPs on the slopes, you'll probably see them on some tropical island, like Virgin Gorda or Antigua (or perhaps one they own that you can't get to). They can also be spotted, in droves, in Palm Beach, Hope Sound, and Captiva Island. The kids are seen wearing neon pink and lime green Lily Pulitzer bathing suits (to help identify them among the natives); the mothers, with too much oil and Jackie O glasses, are reading the latest tell-all book on Lady Di; and the fathers are either playing golf or going through office faxes (sometimes both).

Though WASPs aren't too inclined to try the local cuisine, they're always only too happy to enjoy the local cocktail offerings, dispelling the myth that WASPs are exclusionary toward foreign cultures. Little by little, these fruity potions have begun popping up on the club menu and at private soirees.

MAI TAI COCKTAIL
MAKES 1 DRINK

½   cup fresh squeezed orange juice

1   tablespoon fresh lime juice

¼   cup Mai Tai mix

¼   cup rum

Crushed ice

Orange wedge

Lime wedge

Mix the juices, Mai Tai mix, rum, and ice. Serve with orange and lime wedges.

PIÑA COLADA
MAKES 1 DRINK

Just like at the Half Moon Bay Club.

½   cup pineapple juice

½   cup dark rum

¼   cup coconut cream

Crushed ice

Chunks of pineapple

Blend all liquid ingredients in a blender with ice. Pour into a coconut shell or chilled glass. Serve with pineapple chunks and a paper umbrella.

MANGO-PAPAYA DAIQUIRI
MAKES 1 DRINK

- ¾ cup fresh mango puree
- ¼ cup fresh papaya puree
- ¾ cup light rum
- 2 tablespoons lime juice
- 3 tablespoons granulated sugar

Crushed ice

Blend ingredients until smooth. Serve in a chilled glass with lime wedges.

ST. CROIX BREEZE
MAKES 1 DRINK

- 3 tablespoons rum
- 3 tablespoons vodka
- ¼ cup grapefruit juice
- ¼ cup cranberry juice
- 2 tablespoons fresh orange juice
- 1 lime, squeezed for juice

Mix ingredients well, then serve over ice cubes.

BOXING DAY
LUNCH

Boxing Day is celebrated the day after Christmas. It recognizes the English tradition of—no, not boxing; that most indecorous sport requiring no club membership—rather, the giving of boxes and presents to the help. It is an annual thank-you for all their labor and loyalty, and believe me, WASPs are nowhere without their help. When dealing with WASPs, even the help needs help.

There is always a Boxing Day lunch before a winter nap, followed by a huge black-tie dance where the help is allowed to celebrate their high position and belovedness in the household by serving drinks.

ENGLISH BROWN STEW
SERVES 8–10

We used to serve this every Boxing Day until more and more the plates came back to the pantry full of stew, which was sometimes used as an ashtray. WASPs love putting out their Dunhills on a beautiful Limoge plate.

4	pounds chuck beef, cut in 1-inch cubes	½	cup tomato juice
6	tablespoons all-purpose flour	1	tablespoon Worcestershire sauce
Fat for browning		½	cup chopped onion
1	tablespoon salt	2	cups peeled shallots
2	teaspoons granulated sugar	Carrots, potatoes, celery, chopped in amounts desired	
5	cups boiling water		

Flour the meat and brown in hot fat. Add seasonings, liquids, and the chopped onion and shallots. Cover and simmer for 2 hours. Add vegetables and cook until they and the meat are tender.

CUTTYHUNK CORN PUDDING
SERVES 6

5   eggs

1   pint heavy cream

1   17-ounce can corn kernels

1   17-ounce can creamed corn

3   tablespoons butter, melted

1   cup bread crumbs

Preheat the oven to 350° F.

Beat the eggs in a large bowl. Add the cream and both cans of corn. Place in a 13 x 9-inch glass baking dish. Stir the butter into the bread crumbs and sprinkle on top. Bake for 50 minutes.

SAUCY'S SUNDAY CAKE
SERVES 10–12

This cake is not for everyone, so make sure to have plenty of mint Milanos on hand.

2	eggs	½	cup vegetable oil
1	cup granulated sugar	½	cup water
2	cups all-purpose flour	1	teaspoon vanilla extract
1	teaspoon baking powder	2	apples, peeled and grated
1	teaspoon baking soda	¾	cup chocolate chips
		½	cup chopped walnuts

Preheat the oven to 375° F. Grease and flour a 10-inch Bundt pan.

Mix the eggs and sugar in a bowl. Add the flour, baking powder, baking soda, oil, water, vanilla, and apples. Mix well. Slowly blend in the chocolate and walnuts. Pour the mixture into the cake pan and bake for 50 minutes, or until a tester comes out clean. Cool on a wire rack.

BLESSING OF THE HOUNDS

There's an old joke that goes, "How can you tell who the bride is at a WASP wedding? She's the one kissing the golden retriever."

Dogs are just as important to WASPs as children; the major distinction being that the dogs get to live in the house indefinitely while the kids get shipped off to school for a minimum of eight years. My friend Martha's family almost fell apart when her great Grammy died and left half her estate to her grandchildren and the other half to her King Charles spaniel, Delilah. They weren't so much upset about the money being left to a pet—that was normal to WASPs. They just couldn't figure out what Delilah was going to do with a Fabergé Egg!

The Blessing of the Hounds happens every New Year's Day in the morning, when a Protestant minister blesses the hounds before the hunt. And then, as the dogs socialize in the stables, everyone jaunts up to the big house for a prehunt bite.

ANGUS'S LIVER PÂTÉ
SERVES APPROXIMATELY 20

1   10-ounce can beef consommé

1   envelope unflavored gelatin

8   ounces liver sausage

4   ounces cream cheese

1   ounce (2 tablespoons) dry sherry

1   ounce (2 tablespoons) bourbon
    whiskey

French bread, thinly sliced

Bring consommé to a boil and then add the gelatin; take pot off stove and stir until dissolved. Let cool.

Blend the liver sausage with the cream cheese. Roll paste into a ball and refrigerate until firm.

Add sherry and bourbon to consommé and mix. Pour into 5 5-ounce custard molds. Shape liver paste to fit into mold, then chill until ready to serve. Invert the molds onto a serving dish and serve with French bread slices.

GABBY AND NIKKOS'S IRISH COFFEE

MAKES 1 GLASS

—⚜—

Everyone on the hunt will have a silver mono-grammed flask full of whiskey, but Gabby always gave everyone a big boost before they left. After two of these, you should hear my uncle Johnny blow that horn.

> ¼ cup fine whiskey
>
> 2 tablespoons maple syrup
>
> ½ cup strong brewed coffee
>
> ¼ cup whipped cream

Pour the whiskey and maple syrup into piping hot coffee. Add whipped cream and serve quickly.

HOUND BISCUITS
MAKES 24 BISCUITS

—⚜—

On hunt day, everyone should be treated like royalty. But don't make the mistake my grandfather always made and feed the dogs salmon and caviar—they tend not to run too fast on that.

3	cups whole wheat flour
¼	cup wheat germ

Pinch of salt

4	tablespoons butter, softened
2	eggs
2	tablespoons milk
2	tablespoons beef bouillon
2	tablespoons molasses

Preheat the oven to 375° F. Lightly grease cookie sheets.

Combine the flour, wheat germ, and salt in a large bowl. Cut in the softened butter. Stir in the remaining ingredients and roll into a ball. Add a little water if too dry.

Roll the dough out on a floured board until about ¾ inch thick. Cut into bone shapes and place on cookie sheets. Bake for 20 minutes. Serve when cooled.

A WASP Funeral Supper

There comes a time in a WASP's life when he or she must stand around with a group of other WASPs looking grim, engaging in forced conversation and sipping a stiff drink. No, I'm not talking about a partners' luncheon at the law firm. I'm talking about the WASP funeral. For those uninitiated, the way one can tell a WASP funeral from such a luncheon is simply this: solids at the funeral, pinstripes at the luncheon.

In every small, predominantly WASP town there is a cemetery where generations have been put to rest to frolic with their ancestors. Every family has a different tradition. Some are buried in their pajamas, some in their prep school jackets, or next to their prize horse. I, myself, want to be buried next to my favorite Jack Russell, Waffles.

ROAST PHEASANT WITH BREAD SAUCE

SERVES 25–30

6	pheasants
4	pounds smoked bacon, sliced
6	cups milk
3	yellow onions, peeled and pierced with cloves
6	cups bread crumbs
1¼	pounds butter, melted

Preheat the oven to 400° F.

Clean and pat dry the birds. Wrap bacon slices around them, making sure the breasts are well covered. Roast uncovered for 1 hour.

While the birds are roasting, place the milk in a double boiler with the onions. Cook over low heat for 1 hour, stirring occasionally. Remove the onions and whisk in the bread crumbs. Stir in the melted butter.

Carve the birds and spoon bread mixture over meat.

YORKSHIRE PUDDING
SERVES 8–10

1¼   cups all-purpose flour

3   cups milk

6   eggs, beaten

Salt

Preheat the oven to 475° F.

Mix all ingredients until smooth. Pour drippings from roasting pheasants into a flat pan. Pour in batter and bake for 25 minutes or until puffy and light brown.

GOVERNOR BRADFORD'S CASSEROLE
SERVES 12

12   large sweet potatoes, peeled and chopped

½   cup unsalted butter, softened

1   8-ounce can peeled and pitted apricots, drained

½   cup butter, melted

½   cup honey

¼   cup packed brown sugar

Preheat the oven to 350° F. Butter a 2-quart casserole dish.

Boil sweet potatoes until tender, about 10 minutes. Mash softened butter with the apricots. Spoon the sweet potatoes into the casserole dish. Drizzle with melted butter and honey, then sprinkle with brown sugar on top. Cover and bake for 45 minutes.

CHESTER'S APPLE CRISP
SERVES 8–10

10	Granny Smith apples
1	lemon, squeezed for juice
1	cup all-purpose flour
1	cup packed brown sugar
½	cup butter
2	teaspoons ground cinnamon
½	teaspoon ground nutmeg

Preheat the oven to 375° F.

Wash, peel, and slice the apples. Mix with lemon juice. Butter a 7 x 9-inch glass baking pan and add apples. Mix remaining ingredients well and spread evenly over apples. Bake for 1 hour, or until bubbly.

Epilogue

Requiem for WASP Cuisine

Fret not if some of these dishes come out uncooked, overcooked, burnt, too bland, without flavor, and unsightly; these are some of the signatures of WASP cooking! And everything can be washed down with a martini!

BADER HOWER

ALEXANDRA WENTWORTH is an actress and comedienne who is a *Tonight Show* regular. She has appeared on *Seinfeld* (remember the "Soup Nazi" episode?) and is an alumnus of *In Living Color*, where she worked with Jim Carrey. Her dead-on impersonations of Cher, Cindy Crawford, and Sharon Stone made her a star nobody can recognize. She hails from a long line of Washington blue bloods—and has the trust fund to prove it. Her only qualification for writing this cookbook is that she worked in catering during college (it was a bad year in the stock market) before she pursued the life of an actress (i.e., she was fired from all culinary establishments).